with Annie
and friends

Written & Illustrated by
Mary Wheeler

Copyright © 2016 by Mary Wheeler
for more information visit www.marywheelerstories.com

For those yearning for the freedom
to really dance.

Annie loved to dance and twirl, but she especially loved to twirl. She twirled everywhere she went. Everyone knew when Annie was coming because she always wore her pink tutu when she twirled.

She twirled around her bedroom; she twirled around the kitchen. She twirled in the garden and she twirled down the street. She even twirled across the playground when she had a chance.

Sometimes Annie twirled so fast that she made herself absolutely dizzy. Sometimes she ran into the wall and sometimes she would stumble and fall. Sometimes she would spin like a top and sometimes she landed, Kerplop!

One day Annie decided to twirl at school. She looked around and no one was there, so she began twirling as fast as she could down the hallway. She twirled so fast that she didn't see Arthur coming out of his classroom and she SMASHED right into him. Annie landed on her bottom in a pile of pink fluff and Arthur landed right beside her.

$\mathcal{A}$rthur got up first, dusted himself off, and helped Annie up. "Are you alright?" Arthur asked leaning over. "I'm just fine." Annie answered, annoyed with herself.

She dusted off her pink twirling dress, "I was just dancing and I didn't see you."

"I've heard about you." said Arthur. "You're the girl who loves to dance and twirl everywhere she goes." "Yep, that's me." said Annie with a little smile.

"I'm a dancer too, but my dancing is a lot different than yours. If you're interested, I'll show you what MY dancing looks like." Annie wasn't REALLY interested, but she nodded her head anyway.

Arthur turned on his iPhone and music started to fill the hallway. He began tapping his foot, one and then the other. Soon he was moving his feet and legs up and down and gliding across the floor. His arms moved from side to side as he went and his body swayed back and forth.

His head and shoulders bobbed up and down to the sound of the music. His whole entire body was in motion. Annie had never seen anything like it before. "Gee Whiz!" she said. "Is that really dancing?" "Sure it is." said Arthur. "Watch me and then just start moving."

"But I don't know those steps. I don't know how to dance like that." Annie said, almost starting to cry. "Oh, you don't need to know any special steps. I just make things up depending upon what the music tells me to do. It's something different every time I dance. Just follow what I do at first, then you'll figure it out."

Arthur grabbed Annie's hand and they started moving together around the hallway. Annie's feet moved stiffly beside Arthur's, but he just kept moving. Soon Annie's feet got into the rhythm of the music and she began sliding from side to side, just like Arthur. Her body started to sway back and forth and her arms moved in the air to copy what Arthur was doing.

Soon she was dancing all by herself. She added a spin to her movement and so did Arthur. The smile on their faces grew bigger and bigger as they neared the end of the hallway. They had never had so much fun.

Annie and Arthur finally stopped to catch their breath. They looked around and found that the music had drawn everyone out of their classrooms to watch. Arthur invited all of them to join the fun.

They danced and pranced, twirled, and skipped back down the hallway, through the doors, and outside onto the playground.

The bigger kids offered a helping hand to the younger, shyer ones. Soon the entire playground was filled with school children dancing and sliding, swinging and swaying to the music.

There were no particular steps, but that didn't matter. Some of the children were dancing in circles, some were dancing in lines, some were crisscrossing through the middle of the playground, and others were moving in place.

$\mathcal{A}$nnie looked around to find movements she liked and just copied them. Her whole body was moving. Rather than just twirling, she added other movements to her dance. She was having the time of her life.

Finally the music slowed down and it was time to go home. Annie still wore her pink tutu, but this time she didn't twirl home. This time, she and Arthur just walked home quietly together.

Annie would still twirl, she decided. But she would make her twirling part of the other steps she had learned today. She would move her arms, shake her legs, spin and slide, step and prance, and move in ways she didn't even know yet. Arthur promised to dance with her too.

Annie was tired after all of that dancing.
She waved goodbye to Arthur and with a yawn,
walked the remaining few steps into the house.
She went straight to her bedroom and quickly
fell asleep, dreaming of more dancing
days to come.

Mary and her husband live in an 1894 Japanese Arts and Crafts house which they are restoring to its original charm. They share their magical home with their 2 dogs and with 2 cats, who think they're really dogs without a bark. When she's not writing, Mary enjoys trying new recipes as well as old ones, likes chocolate chip-oatmeal cookies, and is restoring and tending their Japanese gardens.

Click onto her website at www.marywheelerstories.com to find out more about Mary and when new Annie books and other fun stories will be available.

Acknowledgements:

Thank you to my amazing family and friends who shared their sense of entrepreneurship and encouraged me to continue down this new career path. You all have my love and gratitude for being there when I needed you.

A special thank you to my husband Brad for his continued support, Jill Shorrock, the graphic designer who took the original, written on construction paper, and transformed it into the beautiful book you hold in your hands. And to Susan Fox for her guidance in moving the story into a completed book.

www.ingramcontent.com/pod-product-compliance
Lightning Source LLC
Chambersburg PA
CBHW042147290426
44110CB00003B/144